Salahddine Krit

University Education and Training

Salahddine Krit

University Education and Training

Strategic areas

ScienciaScripts

Imprint

Any brand names and product names mentioned in this book are subject to trademark, brand or patent protection and are trademarks or registered trademarks of their respective holders. The use of brand names, product names, common names, trade names, product descriptions etc. even without a particular marking in this work is in no way to be construed to mean that such names may be regarded as unrestricted in respect of trademark and brand protection legislation and could thus be used by anyone.

Cover image: www.ingimage.com

This book is a translation from the original published under ISBN 978-620-7-47989-4.

Publisher:
Sciencia Scripts
is a trademark of
Dodo Books Indian Ocean Ltd. and OmniScriptum S.R.L publishing group

120 High Road, East Finchley, London, N2 9ED, United Kingdom
Str. Armeneasca 28/1, office 1, Chisinau MD-2012, Republic of Moldova, Europe
Printed at: see last page
ISBN: 978-620-0-30389-9

CONTENTS

PREAMBLE

Ibnou Zohr University is one of the largest universities in southern Morocco. It is located in Agadir and covers several towns in the region. The university plays a central role in the development of higher education in the area, covering a wide range of disciplines from science, literature and humanities, to economics, management and law. With its numerous faculties, schools and research centres, Ibnou Zohr University actively contributes to the intellectual, scientific and cultural development of the Souss-Massa region, meeting the country's educational and socio-economic needs.

The Agadir Higher School of Education and Training (ESEF)

As part of the Ibnou Zohr University, the École Supérieure de l'Éducation et de la Formation (ESEF) in Agadir occupies an important place in the Moroccan education system. Created to meet the growing demand for qualified professionals in the field of teaching, the ESEF is dedicated to training competent teachers and educational managers capable of adapting to modern educational reforms and challenges.

The school offers a wide range of courses, from bachelor's to master's degrees, with a particular focus on educational innovation, classroom management and the integration of new technologies into teaching. It is also supported by continuing education programmes to enable practising teachers to update their skills. As an institution attached to Ibnou Zohr University, the Agadir ESEF is committed to training professionals capable of keeping pace with changes in the Moroccan education system, while helping to improve the quality of teaching in the country.

The École Supérieure de l'Éducation et de la Formation (ESEF) in Agadir is a key institution in Morocco, specialising in the training of teachers and education professionals. It aims to improve the education system by offering programmes adapted to today's challenges, both in theory and in practice.

1. Training programmes :

ESEF offers a number of courses covering different levels of education:

- **Bachelor's degree in Education Sciences**: This undergraduate course provides students with a solid grounding in pedagogy, the psychology of learning and educational theory.
- **Master's degree in Education Sciences**: This postgraduate course takes a more in-depth look at subjects such as school management, skills assessment and educational administration. It also trains students in educational reforms and pedagogical innovation.
- **Further training**: For teachers already in post, there are professional training courses to help them improve their skills, particularly in digital teaching and distance learning.

2. Internships and practical immersion :

Students benefit from placements in schools, enabling them to apply theoretical knowledge in a real-life environment. They develop skills in classroom management and in adapting teaching methods to meet students' needs.

3. Commitment to educational reform :

The Agadir ESEF contributes to efforts to modernise the Moroccan education system, in line with the 2015-2030 Strategic Vision. The school is actively involved in reforms aimed at improving the quality of teaching, promoting inclusive education and integrating new technologies into the classroom.

4. Skills developed :

Students acquire a range of professional skills, including :

- **Pedagogical**: Ability to design lessons to suit the pupils, use effective assessment techniques and manage classes to optimum effect.
- **Technological**: mastery of digital tools, distance learning and interactive resources.
- **Relational and organisational**: Effective communication with students, parents and colleagues, time management and lesson planning.

5. Resources and infrastructure :

The school has modern resources to facilitate learning:

- **Interactive classrooms** with digital equipment.
- **Documentation centres** for specialist literature.
- **Teaching laboratories** for simulating teaching situations before testing them out in the field.

6. Job opportunities :

Graduates of ESEF Agadir can enter a variety of careers, such as :

- Teachers in public and public schools, at various levels.
- Managers or educational supervisors.
- Educational advisers, trainers or researchers in the field of education.

The Agadir ESEF trains professionals who are ready to meet the challenges of Morocco's rapidly changing education sector.

The development project for the period 2024-2028 is framed by the Royal Guidelines cited in the following extracts from the speeches of His Majesty King Mohammed VI:

Extracts from speeches by His Majesty King Mohammed VI on National Education, Higher Education, Scientific Research and Innovation

"...The judicious reform of the education and training system is the essential path to take if we are to meet the challenges of development, because we must recognise that this is not simply a question of sectoral reform, but of a salutary struggle in the face of a major challenge. And to achieve this, we have n o choice but to promote research and innovation, and

ensure the upgrading of our human resources, which are our main asset... **(Extract from the speech by His Majesty the King on the occasion of Throne Day, 30 July 2009).**

"...We also expect this governance to contribute to strengthening the foundations of national solidarity and consolidating social justice, which is based on the continued recovery of the education system.
This will require greater awareness of the importance of the progress made in this area, and a better understanding of the long road still ahead.
It is therefore necessary to make constant and sustained efforts and to be firmly convinced of the crucial role of the national school system as a privileged forum for expressing the principle of equal opportunities and introducing the virtues of citizenship, and as an inexhaustible source of resources for human development...". **(Extract from the speech by His Majesty the King at the opening of the 1st Session of the 3rd legislative year, 09 October 2009).**

"...In my opening speech to Parliament, I stressed the need to place youth issues at the heart of the new development model. I also called for the development of an integrated strategy dedicated to young people, which would define the means to effectively promote their status.
Indeed, a young person cannot be called upon to play his role and fulfil his duty without first having benefited from the necessary opportunities and qualifications...".

"... In fact, we must no longer accept that our education system functions as a machine for producing legions of unemployed people, especially in

certain university courses whose graduates, as everyone knows, have enormous difficulty entering the job market...".

"...Furthermore, when a large number of young people, particularly those with advanced degrees in scientific and technical fields, think of emigrating, they are not motivated solely by the tempting incentives of life abroad. They are also considering this possibility because in their own country they lack a climate and conditions favourable to active life, professional advancement, innovation and scientific research...".

" ... We therefore urge the government and the stakeholders concerned to take, as soon as possible, a series of measures aimed in particular at achieving the following objectives:

- First: undertake a comprehensive overhaul of public support mechanisms and programmes for youth employment, to make them more effective and tailored to the expectations of young people. This overhaul must be based on the model I advocated in the Speech from the Throne for social protection programmes...".

"... - Secondly: to give priority to those specialities that will lead to employment and to introduce an effective system of early guidance in the second or third year before the baccalauréat. Its role is to help students, according to their aptitudes and inclinations, to make one of two choices: to embark on a university course or a vocational training course...".

"... - Thirdly: an in-depth review of vocational training specialities to ensure that they meet the needs of businesses and the public sector, and are in step with the changes taking place in the industrial and professional sectors. In this way, graduates will have a better chance of integrating professionally..."

"... - Fourth: Put in place practical mechanisms to improve the quality of incentives for young people to set up small and medium-sized businesses in their specialist fields and to support self-employment initiatives and the creation of social enterprises...".

"... - Fifth: introduce new mechanisms for integrating part of the informal sector into the formal sector, by providing the human potential of the informal sector with appropriate training, incentives and social cover, and by supporting their self-employment or business creation projects...".

"... - Sixth: set up a compulsory programme in each establishment, spread over a period of three to six months, to bring students and trainees up to speed in foreign languages; encourage greater linguistic integration at all levels of study, particularly in the teaching of scientific and technical subjects...

" **(Extract from the speech by His Majesty the King on the occasion of the 65ème anniversary of the Revolution of the King and the People, 20 August 2018).**

VISION

The École Supérieure de l'Éducation et de la Formation (ESEF) in Agadir, as part of Ibnou Zohr University, has set itself the mission of preparing a new generation of teachers and educational managers to meet the demands of modern education in Morocco. In line with the **National Pact for Higher Education, Research and Innovation 2030 (ESRI 2030)**, the Agadir ESEF is committed to meeting the needs of a Moroccan education system in the throes of transformation, by placing innovation and research at the heart of its priorities.

The ESRI 2030 Pact is a strategic roadmap for strengthening the quality, effectiveness and impact of higher education and research in Morocco, by ensuring better links between education, the economy and society. ESEF is fully aligned with this vision, orienting its actions around the main objectives of the pact, including adaptation to new technologies, a focus on 21st^e century skills, and the development of a sustainable and inclusive approach to education.

1. Educational excellence and the development of 21st^e century skills

The Agadir ESEF aspires to train teachers capable of meeting the new demands of the education system, while integrating the skills of the 21^e century such as critical thinking, collaboration, creativity and communication. The main objectives are:

- **Ongoing review of programmes**: The school regularly updates its programmes to incorporate the latest pedagogical developments, technological innovations and global skills that enable teachers to adapt to new learning environments.

• **Training in active pedagogy**: ESEF favours learner-centred teaching approaches, such as project-based learning, problem-solving and collaborative practices, which better prepare future teachers for the modern classroom.

• **Developing digital skills**: Teachers trained at ESEF acquire a solid command of information and communication technologies (ICT), with a focus on the use of digital tools for lesson planning, class management and personalising teaching.

2. Innovation and digital transition

In line with one of the main thrusts of the ESRI 2030 Pact, which emphasises the digitalisation of education, the Agadir ESEF plays a central role in the digital transition of teaching practices. This is reflected in :

• **Promotion of hybrid teaching**: ESEFA incorporates hybrid teaching models (combining face-to-face and online teaching), enabling teachers to manage virtual and physical classes seamlessly. This approach ensures continuity of learning in a variety of contexts, such as exceptional health situations or geographical isolation.

• **Use of learning platforms**: The school uses digital learning environments (LMS) and collaborative platforms to encourage distance learning, while providing personalised, interactive support for students.

• **Innovation laboratories**: ESEFA has technology laboratories where future teachers can experiment with digital tools, educational simulations and interactive software to optimise their teaching skills.

3. Inclusion and equity in education

As part of its vision, ESEFA strives to train teachers who are aware of the importance of inclusiveness in the educational environment. In line with the commitments of the ESRI 2030 Pact, the school promotes :

- **Education for all**: ESEFA aims to ensure that the teachers it trains are able to promote quality education for all students, particularly those from disadvantaged backgrounds, or children with special needs. Specialised training modules are dedicated to inclusive education and managing diversity in the classroom.
- **Raising awareness of gender equality and cultural diversity**: Teacher training emphasises the importance of equal opportunities between the sexes and respect for cultural differences. This aims to encourage a teaching approach that values and celebrates diversity in all its forms.

4. Continuing training and professional development

One of the pillars of the ESRI 2030 Pact is the continuous improvement of the skills of education staff. In response to this, ESEF offers a range of professional training and continuing development courses for practising teachers, focusing on :

- **Improving teaching practices**: Targeted training courses are being set up to enable teachers to update their teaching methods, particularly in the light of changes in teaching methods and technology.
- **Developing educational leadership skills**: Specific modules aim to train educational managers capable of leading schools and steering reforms within their educational communities.

- **Monitoring and evaluation**: The school encourages a culture of continuous self-evaluation, where teachers are trained to evaluate their own practices and adjust their methods according to the results and needs of their pupils.

5. Research and innovation in educational sciences

The Agadir ESEF aims to become a centre of innovation in educational research, in line with the ESRI 2030 Pact's objective of strengthening university research. Its actions in this area include

- **Pedagogical action research**: teacher-researchers are encouraged to conduct applied research that provides practical solutions to the challenges facing the Moroccan education sector, such as reducing school drop-out rates and improving student performance.
- **Collaboration with international institutions**: As part of an international partnership approach, ESEF seeks to collaborate with world-renowned institutions and universities to exchange best practices and pedagogical innovations.

6. Sustainable development and social responsibility

In line with the Sustainable Development Goals (SDGs) promoted by the ESRI 2030 Pact, ESEF integrates sustainability principles into its educational programmes and practices. The school is committed to:

- **Training teachers to be aware of environmental issues**: Future teachers are made aware of the importance of integrating environmental and sustainability issues into their teaching, in order to prepare generations of aware and responsible pupils.

- **Promoting a sustainable approach to resources**: ESEF encourages the sustainable management of educational resources, adopting practices that minimise the ecological footprint of schools, in particular through digitisation and the reduction of paper use.

7. Partnerships and international cooperation

To reinforce the impact of its actions, ESEF Agadir actively participates in national and international partnerships which contribute to :

- **Exchanging experience and best practice**: Through collaborations with universities and international organisations, the school is able to take advantage of global best practice and adapt it to the Moroccan context.

- **Facilitating international mobility for students and teachers**: Mobility programmes, in collaboration with partner institutions, enable teachers and students to benefit from international experience and enrich their educational careers through exposure to foreign educational methods and systems.

The vision of the Agadir ESEF, aligned with the objectives of the **ESRI 2030 Pact**, is based on excellence, innovation and social responsibility. It aspires to train a new generation of teachers and educational leaders capable of accompanying educational reforms, while meeting the challenges of the digital transition and education for all. This ambitious vision is part of a dynamic of continuous transformation of the Moroccan education system, in line with the global challenges of the 21e century.

Current status of ESEFA

1. Educational

Advantages :

- **In-service teacher training** : ESEFA sets up training programmes to improve teachers' teaching skills in science and mathematics. This makes it possible to introduce more modern and effective teaching methods.

- **Interactive and personalised learning**: The use of digital tools allows students to progress at their own pace, making education more accessible and tailored to each student profile. Simulations, videos and interactive media help to clarify complex concepts, making learning more dynamic.

Disadvantages :

- **Resistance to pedagogical change**: Some teachers, particularly those used to traditional methods, find it difficult to adopt new technologies and pedagogical approaches.

- **Lack of in-depth training**: Although training is offered, some regions suffer from a lack of adequate support to ensure that teachers are sufficiently prepared to effectively integrate digital tools into their teaching.

- **Disparities in access**: Urban schools are often better equipped than rural schools, exacerbating educational inequalities between different areas.

2. Scientists

Advantages :

- **Encouraging local research**: The programme encourages local scientific research by encouraging students to solve real problems encountered in their environment, thereby strengthening problem-solving and innovation skills.
- **Access to global resources**: Students and teachers can access an international database and scientific resources, updating knowledge and broadening educational perspectives.

Disadvantages :

- **Lack of physical facilities**: Although digital tools are very useful for theoretical learning, many institutions do not have adequate facilities for scientific practice, such as laboratories.
- **Inadequate simulations**: Virtual simulations do not always replace laboratory experiments, particularly in the experimental sciences where manual work and direct interaction with physical materials are crucial.

3. Infrastructure

Advantages :

- **Digitisation of educational resources**: ESEFA promotes the digitisation of teaching materials, enabling wider distribution at reduced cost. This helps teachers and students to have access to diversified and up-to-date content without the material constraints associated with physical textbooks.

- **Improving digital infrastructure**: The programme encourages investment in digital school infrastructure (computers, Internet connection), particularly in less developed areas.

Disadvantages :

- **Limited access to digital infrastructure**: Rural and isolated areas often suffer from a lack of reliable Internet connection, which considerably limits the impact of the programme in these regions. This creates a digital divide between urban and rural areas.
- **Costly maintenance**: The cost of acquiring and maintaining digital tools (computers, tablets, software, Internet connection) is often prohibitive for schools in developing countries. Electricity supply is also a problem in some regions, rendering technological tools unusable.
- **Dependence on technology**: In the absence of electricity or Internet, education can be disrupted. This highlights an over-reliance on technological infrastructure, which is not always stable in some regions.

Conclusion

ESEFA is a programme with laudable ambitions that is making a major contribution to modernising science teaching and improving scientific research in Africa. However, the success of this programme depends heavily on the ability to reduce disparities in digital infrastructure, strengthen teacher training and overcome technological limitations in disadvantaged regions.

STRATEGY & APPROACH

Strategy of the École Supérieure de l'Éducation et de la Formation (ESEF) in Agadir

The strategy of the Agadir ESEF is designed to meet the challenges of the Moroccan education system and to train teachers capable of implementing the necessary reforms. It focuses on several key areas:

1. Continuous improvement of training quality

ESEF focuses on the quality of its training to ensure that its graduates are well prepared for the job market. Specific measures include:

- **External evaluation of programmes**: External experts are regularly invited to evaluate ESEF's training programmes to ensure that they are in line with international standards and the expectations of the education market.

- **Establishment of advisory boards**: A board made up of education professionals, former students and employers is set up to advise on the development of programmes and teaching practices.

- **Teacher training**: ESEF invests in the ongoing training of its teachers, offering them professional development opportunities to keep them up to date with the latest pedagogical trends and innovations in the field of education.

2. Developing digital skills

Digitising education is a priority for ESEF. To this end, a number of initiatives have been put in place:

- **Creation of digital educational resources**: Teachers are encouraged to create and share digital educational resources adapted to different learning levels. This includes educational videos, infographics and interactive educational games.

- **Training in digital tools**: Practical workshops are organised to train teachers in the use of various digital tools such as learning management platforms (LMS), online collaboration tools and educational applications.

- **Encouraging innovation**: Teachers are encouraged to use innovative teaching methods that incorporate new technologies, such as flipped classes, virtual simulations and mobile learning.

3. Strengthening educational research capacity

ESEF strives to become a hub for educational research, with a focus on:

- **Collaborative research projects**: The school encourages teachers and students to collaborate on research projects that examine issues specific to the Moroccan education system, such as the effectiveness of new teaching methods or the impact of digital resources on learning.

- **Publications and dissemination of results**: The results of research carried out at ESEF are published in academic journals, and conferences are organised to share best practice and research results with the education community.

- **Encouraging action research**: Teachers are trained to carry out action research in their classrooms, enabling them to apply their findings directly to their teaching practice.

4. Promoting inclusive and equitable education

ESEF is committed to promoting equitable and inclusive education. Initiatives include:

- **Diversity management training**: Specific modules are integrated into the teacher training curriculum to prepare teachers to manage heterogeneous classes, taking into account cultural and socio-economic differences and the special needs of pupils.
- **Support for pupils in difficulty**: ESEF develops specific support programmes to help future teachers work with pupils with special educational needs, particularly those with disabilities or who are failing at school.
- **Creating an inclusive learning environment**: The school puts in place practices and policies to ensure that all students, regardless of background or ability, have access to a quality education.

5. Internationalisation and partnerships

ESEF values national and international partnerships to enrich its programmes. Initiatives include:

- **Cooperation agreements with other institutions** : ESEF establishes agreements with universities and educational organisations abroad to exchange experience, teaching resources and teaching practices.
- **Exchange and mobility programmes**: ESEF facilitates the mobility of students and teachers through exchange programmes, enabling participants to discover new educational approaches and enrich their professional experience.

- **Participation in international education networks**: ESEF is involved in education networks to collaborate on projects, share resources and participate in international education conferences.

Approach taken by the École Supérieure de l'Éducation et de la Formation (ESEF) in Agadir

ESEF's pedagogical approach focuses on active learning, inclusiveness, and the personal and professional development of future teachers. Key aspects of this approach include:

1. Skills-based approach

This approach focuses on developing the practical and analytical skills of future teachers:

- **Collaborative projects**: Students work in teams on real projects that simulate classroom situations, developing skills in communication, collaboration and project management.
- **Performance-based assessments**: Instead of traditional examinations, ESEF uses performance-based assessments, where students demonstrate their skills through presentations, workshops and peer assessments.
- **Critical reflection and self-assessment**: Future teachers are encouraged to reflect on their practices and to self-assess, which helps them to identify their strengths and weaknesses and to draw up personal development plans.

2. Student-centred and inclusive approach

ESEF focuses on student-centred teaching, fostering an inclusive learning environment:

- **Differentiated teaching**: Teachers are trained to adapt their teaching methods to meet the diverse learning styles and specific needs of their students, incorporating a variety of activities that engage all learners.
- **Use of assistive technology**: ESEF trains teachers to use assistive technology to support students with disabilities, enabling them to participate fully in school activities.
- **Community involvement**: Students are encouraged to get involved with their community by taking part in service projects, enabling them to develop social skills while contributing to society.

3. Experiential learning

ESEF values experiential learning, where students are involved in real teaching situations:

- **Work placements in schools**: Future teachers spend a significant part of their training in schools, where they put into practice the skills they have learnt and are supervised by experienced teachers.
- **Practical workshops**: ESEF organises workshops where students can experiment with different teaching methods and receive constructive feedback on their performance.
- **Meetings with education professionals**: The school regularly invites educators and specialists to share their experiences and discuss current issues in education, thereby enriching students' training.

These integrated strategies and approaches aim to equip future teachers with the skills and knowledge they need to thrive in a constantly changing educational environment, while meeting the requirements of the ESRI 2030 Pact and the expectations of Moroccan society.

Strategic Area I :

Strengthening the training offer and Educational Innovation,

For this axis and in the current development project for Hassan II University in Casablanca, we propose a series of specific priority teaching objectives for each type of training:

- Initial training ;
- Continuing education ;
- Distance learning.

INITIAL TRAINING :

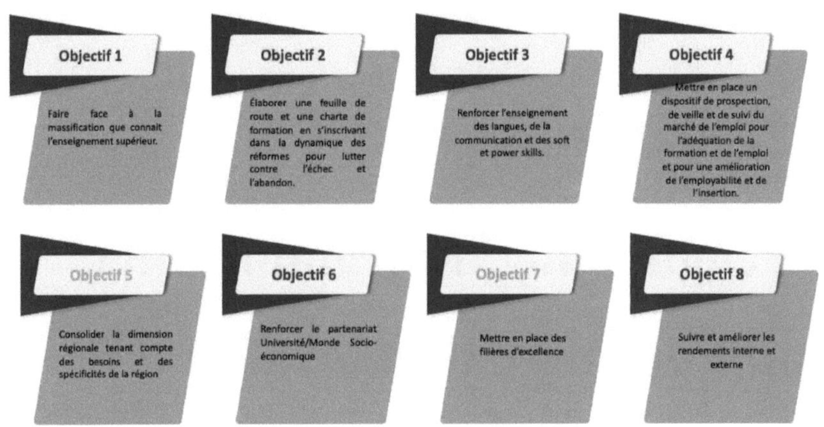

CONTINUING EDUCATION :

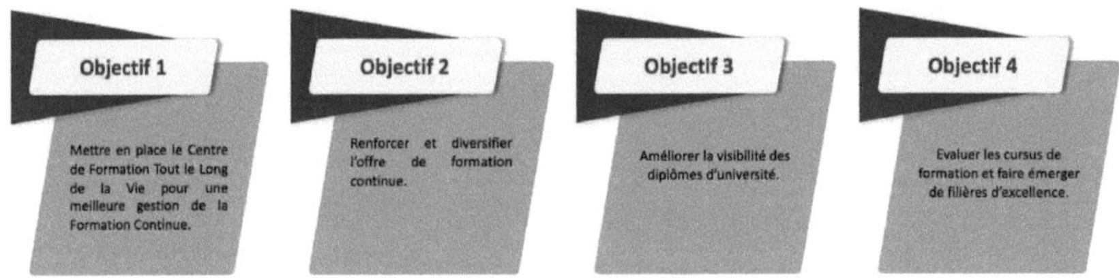

DISTANCE LEARNING

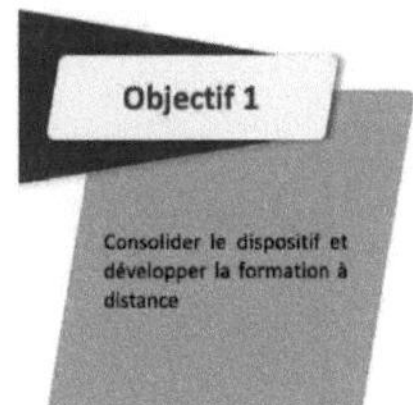

Main objective: To

adapt and improve the training on offer, taking into account the current and future needs of the education sector in Morocco, by integrating innovative and inclusive teaching approaches, while meeting regional, national and international requirements.

1. Diversification and Alignment of Training Programmes with Sector Needs

Specific objectives :

- Create programmes that meet the growing needs in inclusive education, special education and managing diversity in the classroom.
- Offer modular and specialised courses in key subjects (science, maths, languages) to strengthen teachers' didactics.
- Incorporate in-service training options with recognised certification for existing teachers.

Concrete actions:

- **Audit of training needs:** Organise consultation workshops with education stakeholders (ministry, schools, local associations) to identify specific training needs.
- **Creation of new curricula:** Developing and offering specialised courses based on the country's educational priorities: digital education, inclusion of children with special needs, teacher training in rural areas.
- **Strengthening work placements:** Requiring long-term placements in pilot schools or partner training establishments to ensure practical immersion for student teachers.

Performance indicators :

- Number of new programmes developed.
- Enrolment rates for new courses.
- Partnerships formed with schools and companies to set up internships.

2. Integration of innovative teaching methods

Specific objectives :

- Promoting active learning and the use of educational technologies for more personalised and interactive teaching.
- Train teachers in the use of digital tools (MOOCs, e-learning platforms, educational software) to support blended learning.
- Encourage experimentation with and adaptation of innovative teaching methods such as flipped classes and project-based learning.

Concrete actions:

- **Creation of online training modules:** Developing interactive content in collaboration with educational technology experts to integrate online courses into existing programmes.
- **Setting up teaching laboratories:** Creating teaching experimentation areas for teachers, equipped with augmented and virtual reality (AR/VR) technologies to simulate classroom environments.
- **In-service training for trainers in educational innovation:** Organise regular seminars for teachers to familiarise them with modern teaching methods and technological innovations in education.

Performance indicators :

- Number of teachers trained in new educational technologies.
- Student use of digital learning platforms.
- Student and teacher evaluation of the new teaching methods introduced.

3. Strengthening in-service training for teachers

Specific objectives :

- Provide in-service training for existing teachers so that they can update their teaching skills in line with new educational methods and curriculum reforms.
- Offer professional support through mentoring for young teachers to improve their teaching practice.

Concrete actions:

- **Planning regular training cycles: Set** up a certified in-service training programme, compulsory for practising teachers, with modules on pedagogical innovation, classroom management and inclusion.
- **Creation of mentoring programmes:** Assign experienced mentors to new teachers to help them overcome the challenges of classroom teaching and adopt effective teaching strategies.
- **Evaluation and monitoring of trained teachers:** Implement evaluation and feedback tools to measure the impact of in-service training on teaching practices.

Performance indicators :

- Rate of teacher participation in in-service training.
- Increase in positive post-training teacher evaluations.
- Number of teachers involved in mentoring programmes.

4. Improving Teaching Infrastructure and Resources

Specific objectives :

- Modernising training infrastructures to support interactive teaching and digital learning.
- Creating greater access to digital educational resources and online libraries to facilitate research and teaching.

Concrete actions:

- **Classroom equipment:** Install interactive whiteboards, video projectors and digital resources in all classrooms to facilitate multimedia teaching.
- **Setting up a digital library:** Creating a digital portal with access to teaching resources (research articles, e-books, specialist journals) for students and teachers.
- **Improving Internet connections:** Ensuring that ESEF has a high quality Internet connection to facilitate the use of online tools by students and teachers.

Performance indicators :

- Number of classrooms equipped with modern technology.
- Frequency of use of the digital library by students and teachers.

- Increased use of e-learning platforms.

5. Developing national and international partnerships

Specific objectives :

- Strengthen collaboration with universities, training centres and businesses to pool resources and create training courses that are better adapted to market needs.
- Develop international exchanges to expose teachers and students to innovative teaching practices.

Concrete actions:

- **Collaboration agreements with other universities:** Signing partnership agreements with Moroccan and international universities and training centres to facilitate exchanges of teachers and students.
- **Participation in collaborative research projects:** Encourage teachers to take part in action research projects in partnership with other institutions, in order to explore new teaching methods and improve teaching.
- **Organisation of international conferences:** Invite international experts to conferences on educational innovations so that teachers and students can benefit from their experiences and practices.

Performance indicators :

- Number of partnerships formed with national and international institutions.
- Participation rate in collaborative research projects.

- Number of conferences organised and experts invited.

This strategic axis aims to transform the ESEF Agadir into a reference institution for pedagogical innovation and teacher training, by integrating local, national and global needs into its training offer. By strengthening its infrastructure, diversifying its programmes and supporting continuous innovation, the ESEF will be able to train teachers capable of meeting the educational challenges of the future, while taking account of the socio-cultural characteristics of the Souss-Massa region.

Strategic Area II :

Innovative scientific research: Visibility and competitiveness of the university

The action plan we are proposing for the development of scientific research at UH2C is based on the following six objectives:

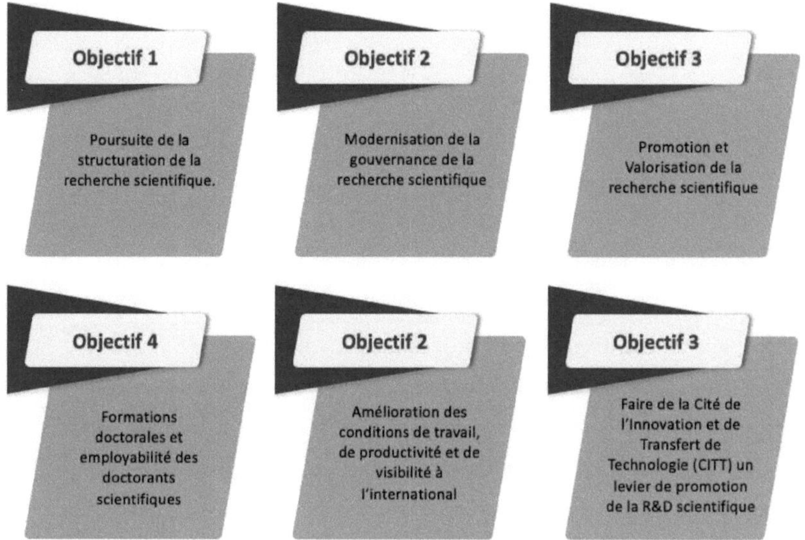

Main objective:

To make ESEF a centre of excellence for scientific research in the field of education, recognised for its innovation, its contribution to pedagogical advances, and its collaboration with national and international partners.

1. Developing and strengthening scientific research capacities

Specific objectives :

- Create a research ecosystem within ESEF to foster a culture of innovation and high-level scientific publication.

- Develop specialist research centres in strategic areas of education (digital teaching, school inclusion, science teaching, etc.).

Concrete actions:

- **Creating an educational research centre:** Setting up a research centre dedicated to current educational issues, with multidisciplinary teams working on themes such as new pedagogical approaches, the use of technology in the classroom, and inclusive education.
- **Research training programme for lecturer-researchers:** Organise methodological training to enhance the research skills of lecturer-researchers (research methods, scientific writing, project management).
- **Acquiring research tools:** Investing in specialist software (such as NVivo for qualitative analysis or SPSS for statistical analysis) to facilitate researchers' work.
- **Setting up research committees:** Setting up research groups in priority areas such as technology-enhanced learning, inclusive education and pedagogical innovation.

Performance indicators :

- Number of research projects launched and funded.
- Number of teacher-researchers who have received methodological training.
- Publications in indexed scientific journals, measured on an annual basis.

2. Creation of National and International Collaboration Networks

Specific objectives :

- To position ESEF as a key player in educational research by forging solid partnerships with academic and research institutions in Morocco and abroad.
- Facilitating the exchange of knowledge and expertise through interdisciplinary and international collaboration.

Concrete actions:

- **Partnerships with international universities and research institutes:** Sign collaboration agreements with recognised universities (e.g. Sorbonne University, Oxford University, etc.) for joint projects, researcher exchanges and joint publications.
- **Participation in research consortia:** Joining regional and international research consortia, such as Horizon Europe or ERASMUS+, to access research funding and strengthen international collaboration.
- **Organisation of scientific conferences:** Launch an annual scientific conference at ESEF to bring together international experts and education researchers to discuss the latest trends and innovations in education.
- **Researcher exchange programmes:** Set up exchange programmes to enable teacher-researchers to collaborate with research teams abroad, while welcoming international researchers to ESEF.

Performance indicators :

- Number of collaborations with international institutions.
- Number of research projects co-financed by foreign or international institutions.
- Number of exchanges of researchers (incoming and outgoing).

3. Promotion and enhancement of scientific research

Specific objectives :

- To increase the visibility of ESEF's research work through scientific promotion and dissemination activities.
- Ensuring the transfer of research results to the education sector to have a direct impact on teaching practices.

Concrete actions:

- **Creation of a scientific journal specific to ESEF:** Launch an indexed scientific journal, published twice a year, to promote the research of teachers and students on innovative educational themes.
- **Disseminating research via an online platform:** Setting up a digital platform where research results can be published and shared with the general public, academic institutions and policy-makers.
- **Active participation in national and international conferences:** Encourage teacher-researchers to submit their work to international conferences to raise their profile and encourage academic exchanges.
- **Development of impact reports:** Publish annual reports on the impact of ESEF research on national education policies and local teaching practices.

Performance indicators :

- Number of articles published in indexed international journals.
- Number of downloads and citations of articles on the online platform.
- Participation in international conferences and citation rates for ESEF researchers.

4. Encouraging applied research and technology transfer

Specific objectives :

- Encouraging applied research to provide practical solutions to regional and national educational issues.
- Develop innovative technological solutions that improve educational practices, such as digital tools and educational platforms.

Concrete actions:

- **Creating laboratories for educational experimentation:** Setting up laboratories for educational innovation where teachers can test and develop new educational approaches, in conjunction with new technologies.

- **Launching research-action projects:** Mobilising researchers and teachers to carry out research-action projects on local issues, such as managing diversity in the classroom or integrating children with disabilities.
- **Collaborations with EdTech companies:** Forging partnerships with local and international technology companies to co-develop innovative teaching tools based on research findings.
- **Incubator for innovative educational projects:** Create an incubator to support entrepreneurial initiatives by researchers and students wishing to develop technological solutions for education.

Performance indicators :

- Number of applied research projects developed and tested in schools.
- Number of innovative teaching tools co-developed with technology companies.
- Number of incubated projects resulting in concrete educational solutions.

5. Support and supervision of young researchers

Specific objectives :

- Training a new generation of education researchers, while supporting them in their academic and professional development.
- Provide resources, mentoring and publication opportunities for doctoral students and young researchers.

Concrete actions:

- **Creation of research grants:** Allocate specific grants to doctoral students and young researchers to support them financially in their research work.
- **Organisation of methodological seminars and workshops:** offering practical training in research methodology, scientific writing and data analysis tools to strengthen the skills of young researchers.

- **Personalised doctoral supervision:** Create thesis management teams to support doctoral students in producing high-quality work, while encouraging collaboration between young researchers and experienced lecturers.
- **Publication support:** Encouraging and helping young researchers to publish their work in recognised scientific journals, in particular through co-publications with senior researchers.

Performance indicators :

- Number of doctoral students funded by research grants.
- Number of scientific publications co-authored by young researchers.
- Success rate of supervised doctoral students.

This detailed **Strategic Area II** aims to transform ESEF into a leader in scientific research in education. Thanks to a policy of research capacity building, international collaboration and the promotion of scientific work, ESEF will be able to establish itself as a key player in educational innovation.

Strategic Area III :

University governance : Responsibility and Mobilisation to support development of the University

A university's overall performance is necessarily multidimensional, since it involves the development of its human resources, the quality of its governance, the relevance of its funding and its range of courses, as well as the effectiveness of its teaching models.

With the aim of improving efficiency in the management of universities and strengthening transparency and accountability, the organisation chart of universities and university establishments was adopted by the joint decision of 9 March 2020 between the Ministry responsible and the Ministry of the Economy, Finance and Administrative Reform. As a result of this decision, the UH2C now has an organisation chart for the university presidency and organisation charts for the university establishments.

In the UH2C's development project for the period 2022-2026, the governance of the UH2C is a fundamental axis for steering within a framework of autonomy, responsibility and accountability in compliance with the Moroccan Code of Good Governance Practices and on the basis of the framework law 51-17 which supports the strategic vision of the higher education sector.

This priority is based on six specific objectives:

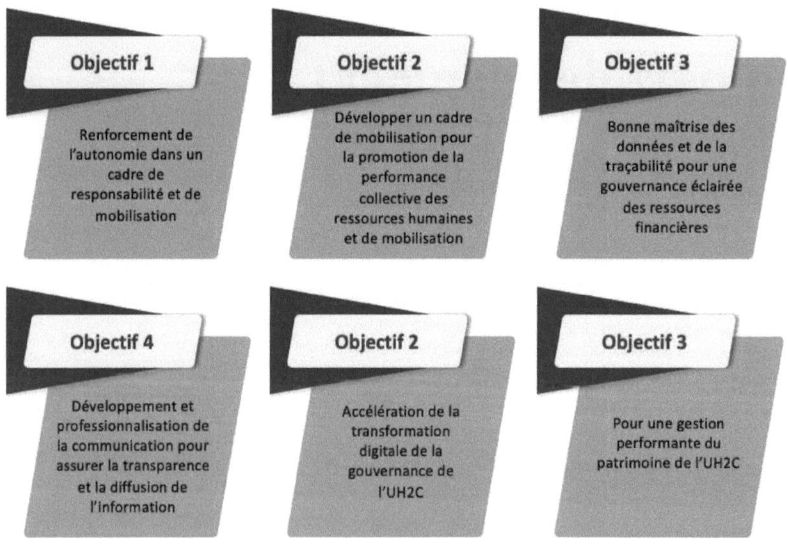

1. Modernising governance and management processes

Modern governance is based on flexible and efficient structures, ensuring the institution's responsiveness to changes in the education sector. Transparent and participatory management encourages rapid and inclusive decision-making, while ensuring compliance with international standards.

Specific objectives :

• Put in place a governance structure that is flexible, transparent and adapted to the new challenges facing higher education.

• Improve administrative efficiency by digitising and automating internal processes.

Detailed actions:

• **Restructuring governance bodies:** Review the composition and roles of decision-making bodies (faculty councils, academic committees, etc.) to improve their effectiveness. Each body should include representatives of faculty, staff, students and external partners to ensure inclusive governance.

• **Implementation of a University Management Information System (SIGU):** Integrating a SIGU to automate administrative processes such as enrolment management, grades, research results and human resources management, in order to improve productivity and reduce administrative delays.

• **Transparency in decision-making:** Develop an online portal accessible to teachers and students to track important decisions, strategic plans and the institution's performance. This will foster a culture of transparency in the management of resources and projects.

Performance indicators :

• Reduced processing times for administrative requests.

• Rate of adoption of digital tools by administrative and academic staff.

- Number of decisions taken in consultation with all stakeholders.

2. Strengthening Corporate Social Responsibility (CSR)

ESEF must assume a leadership role in social and environmental responsibility. By integrating sustainable development principles into its operations, the institution can position itself as a key player in educational and societal sustainability.

Specific objectives :

- Integrating sustainable practices into the day-to-day management of the institution.
- Promote social responsibility within ESEF and with its partners.

Detailed actions:

- **University Green Plan:** Develop a plan to reduce ESEF's ecological footprint (waste management, energy consumption, green spaces on campus, etc.), including the establishment of long-term sustainability objectives.
- **Raising awareness of social and environmental issues:** Launch awareness campaigns on resource management, sustainable practices and civic engagement to actively involve students, teachers and staff.
- **Development of community projects:** Encourage students to take part in community projects aimed at improving local social conditions (literacy, access to education for disadvantaged children, etc.).

Performance indicators :

- Reduction in energy consumption and waste produced by ESEF.
- Number of community projects and social initiatives launched by students.
- Involvement of students and staff in CSR awareness-raising initiatives.

3. Mobilising Stakeholders for Collaborative Development

The involvement of internal and external stakeholders is essential to the development and implementation of ESEF's strategic vision. This includes not only academic and administrative staff, but also students, external partners (companies, local authorities, NGOs) and alumni.

Specific objectives :

- Engage all ESEF stakeholders in a collaborative process of institutional development.
- Strengthen strategic partnerships to align ESEF programmes with the needs of the market and local stakeholders.

Detailed actions:

- **Creation of an external advisory committee:** Form a committee of partners from the professional world, education and the public sector to guide the strategic direction of ESEF, while ensuring the relevance of the training programmes.
- **Involvement of alumni:** Develop a platform for interaction with alumni so that they can play a role in supporting new graduates (coaching, mentoring, internship and job offers).
- **Participatory innovation forums:** Organise regular workshops and discussion forums with stakeholders to assess educational needs and identify opportunities for pedagogical innovation.

Performance indicators :

- Number of partnerships formed with local businesses and institutions.
- Alumni participation in ESEF events.
- Number of projects co-developed with external stakeholders.

4. Training and Capacity Building in Leadership and Management

The ongoing training of administrative and academic staff is a crucial element in ensuring the effective management of the institution. By developing a culture of leadership and proactive management, ESEF will be better able to adapt to the changing demands of the education sector.

Specific objectives :

- Train ESEF managers in strategic management and leadership practices.
- Promoting a culture of innovation and participative management to optimise the governance of the institution.

Detailed actions:

- **Leadership training programmes:** Offering training in project management, change management and leadership for academic and administrative staff.
- **Internal and external mentoring:** Encourage mentoring initiatives, where the most experienced managers support young leaders in their professional development, with the possibility of including external mentors from various sectors.
- **Innovation in academic management:** Create internal working groups to encourage innovation in academic and administrative management, adopting participative practices that empower teams.

Performance indicators :

- Number of managers who have taken part in leadership training.
- Staff and teacher satisfaction with management practices.
- Number of innovative management initiatives implemented.

5. Monitoring and Continuous Performance Evaluation

Monitoring and evaluation of the actions undertaken are necessary to adjust ESEF's development strategy and ensure continuous improvement in academic, administrative and institutional performance.

Specific objectives :

- Put in place transparent evaluation mechanisms to measure progress and adjust actions according to results.
- Fostering a culture of continuous improvement to optimise the institution's performance.

Detailed actions:

- **Creating monitoring dashboards:** Developing dashboards incorporating key performance indicators (KPIs) to monitor the results of strategic projects, research, human resources management and academic performance in real time.
- **Internal and external audits:** Conducting regular audits to assess the quality of internal processes, identify areas for improvement and ensure compliance with international standards.
- **Rapid adjustment mechanisms:** Develop mechanisms to react quickly to the results of evaluations and audits, adapting strategies accordingly.

Performance indicators :

- Rate of achievement of strategic objectives.
- Number of audit recommendations implemented.
- Continuous improvement in performance indicators from year to year.

Conclusion

Strategic Area III is part of an overall process of modernisation and institutional accountability, aimed at making ESEF Agadir an institution of excellence in university governance. By promoting inclusive decision-making, strong social responsibility and active collaboration with stakeholders, this strategic area will enable ESEF to position itself as a model of participatory and sustainable governance.

Strategic Area IV :

Strengthening cooperation, Orverture and Partnerships,

UH2C is a university that is open to its regional and national socio-economic environment, which gives it a strong role to play in the dynamism of the region and the country. It also has an international outlook, giving the international dimension a key role to play.

Our strategy will be based on consolidating the university's achievements in terms of partnerships and cooperation. A great deal of work has gone into establishing relationships and carrying out actions with various partners. We will be updating and evaluating current agreements, while strengthening existing cooperative relationships and forging new links at regional, national and international level.

The action plan is broken down into four specific objectives:

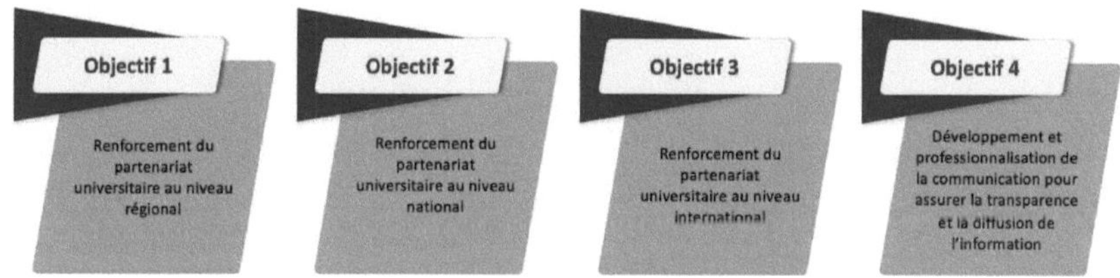

1. Strengthening national and international academic partnerships

The development of academic partnerships is a priority for ESEF in order to promote solid educational and scientific collaboration. These partnerships encourage the exchange of knowledge, innovation in teaching approaches, and provide students with diversified study prospects.

Additional objectives:

• To create a network of scientific and educational collaboration between ESEF and other universities in Morocco, Africa and the rest of the world.

• Adapting training programmes to international standards by benefiting from the best practices of partner institutions.

Additional detailed actions :

• **Participation in international research and development (R&D) programmes:** ESEF could participate in joint research projects funded by international organisations, such as the European Union (Horizon Europe programme), or UNESCO, to address global educational issues such as inclusive education, technology in education, and sustainable education.

• **Joint training courses and workshops with partners:** Develop short training courses, workshops and joint seminars with partner universities on emerging themes (artificial intelligence in education, sustainable development, digital education).

• **Creation of a virtual learning platform:** Collaborating with other institutions to create a multilingual online learning platform that facilitates exchanges between students and teachers from different partner institutions, while offering internationally recognised joint qualifications.

Additional performance indicators :

- Number of joint scientific publications with international partners.
- Number of research projects funded by international organisations involving ESEF.
- Rate of teacher participation in training courses or workshops with partner institutions.

2. Partnerships with the Private and Public Sectors

Collaboration with the private sector and public institutions is a strategic lever for ESEF, as it allows us to better adapt our courses to the needs of the labour market and to facilitate the professional integration of our students.

Additional objectives:

• Diversify funding sources for ESEF's educational and research projects through public-private partnerships.

• To strengthen the match between ESEF's training offer and the needs of companies in emerging sectors such as technology, innovation and sustainable development.

Additional detailed actions :

• **Creation of teaching chairs sponsored by companies:** Set up chairs of excellence in partnership with local or international companies in strategic areas (e.g. educational innovation, educational technologies). These chairs would make it possible to fund applied research projects, advanced training courses and academic events.

• **Development of centres of excellence in partnership with the public sector:** Work with local authorities and government departments to create centres of excellence specialising in education, social innovation and inclusion. These centres could serve as platforms for the development of community projects, applied research and the improvement of public policy in education.

- **Creation of an observatory of labour market trends:** Set up an observatory in collaboration with local and regional economic players to identify skills in high demand and adjust training programmes accordingly.

Additional performance indicators :

- Amount of funding obtained by companies and public institutions for ESEF projects.
- Number of teaching chairs created in collaboration with companies.
- Number of internships and job opportunities offered to students through partnerships with the private sector.

3. Cooperation with NGOs and International Organisations

Cooperation with NGOs and international organisations is essential to position ESEF as a key player in the field of education, particularly in the context of development and inclusive education.

Additional objectives:

• Strengthen ESEF's role in international Education for All projects, with a particular focus on rural areas and vulnerable populations.

• Benefit from the expertise of NGOs to introduce innovative and inclusive teaching methods.

Additional detailed actions :

• **Inclusive education projects with international NGOs:** Collaborate with organisations such as UNICEF and UNESCO to develop education projects that promote access to education for disadvantaged children and adults, particularly in rural areas of Morocco. These projects could include awareness-raising campaigns, teacher training and the integration of new educational technologies.

• **Training teachers in inclusive education methods:** In partnership with specialist NGOs, provide training for teachers on inclusive education, with a focus on pupils with disabilities, children from disadvantaged backgrounds, and girls' education in rural areas.

• **Participation in international education forums and networks:** Involve ESEF in international forums to share good practice and participate actively in global discussions on inclusive education, sustainable development and pedagogical innovation.

Additional performance indicators :

- Number of educational projects carried out with international NGOs.

- Number of inclusive education training courses organised in collaboration with partners.

- Measurable impact on access to education in rural areas and for vulnerable populations.

4. Promoting ESEF's International Visibility

To strengthen its international reputation, ESEF needs to put in place a global strategy for communication and international visibility. This includes organising international events, promoting scientific publications and attracting foreign students and teachers.

Additional objectives:

- To strengthen ESEF's international reputation as an institution of excellence in education and training.
- Develop targeted communication initiatives to attract foreign talent (teachers, students, researchers).

Additional detailed actions :

- **Launch of scholarships for international students:** Create specific scholarship programmes to attract students from African countries, Europe and other regions, thereby strengthening cultural diversity within ESEF.
- **Creation of an international academic journal:** Launch a scientific journal published by ESEF focusing on innovations in education and training, with contributions from international researchers. This journal could contribute to increasing the academic visibility of ESEF.
- **Active participation in international accreditation networks:** Integrate ESEF into international accreditation networks to ensure that its programmes meet global standards and to facilitate international recognition of the diplomas awarded.

Additional performance indicators :

- Number of international students enrolled on scholarships.
- Number of publications and articles in international journals.
- Number of international academic collaborations recognised by accreditation networks.

5. Creating synergies between research, training and partnerships

Synergies between research, training and partnerships enable us to capitalise on the strengths of each sector to create innovations that meet the needs of the market and society. This also helps to integrate students more effectively into the socio-economic fabric.

Additional objectives:

- Develop interdisciplinary training programmes linked to applied research projects.
- Encourage student participation in collaborative research projects with industrial and institutional partners.

Additional detailed actions :

- **Developing entrepreneurial projects with students:** Create an incubation programme to enable students to develop innovative projects in conjunction with private partners, while benefiting from the support of mentors from the academic and entrepreneurial worlds.
- **Setting up action research programmes:** Encouraging students to take part in action research programmes with companies, NGOs and public institutions to solve concrete problems linked to education, sustainable development or social inclusion.

Additional performance indicators :

- Number of entrepreneurial projects launched by students in collaboration with companies.

- Number of action research programmes involving students and partners.
- Rate of integration of research results into training programmes.

Conclusion

Strengthening cooperation, openness and partnerships is a strategic opportunity for ESEF Agadir to position itself as a key player in educational innovation on a global scale. By developing solid relationships with academic, industrial, public and international partners, ESEF can not only strengthen its training and research programmes, but also improve its overall impact on society and the economy of Morocco and the MENA region.

Strategic Area V :

University life and inclusion,

The university is a civic space. It must play an active role in the life of the region and the local area, and campuses must now be recognised as open and lively places. In this project, we want to emphasise the need to recognise the university's role in local development, whether from an economic, environmental or social point of view.

Socialisation is a major challenge for students, and goes hand in hand with the fight against isolation. Socialisation is a cross-cutting factor in well-being. Particularly for students.

In the UH2C development project for the period 2022-2026, university life and inclusion are supported by the projects of framework law 51-17 (Project 10: Development of University Life and Project 11: Development of University Sport) which supports our nation's strategic vision of education.

This theme is based on four specific objectives:

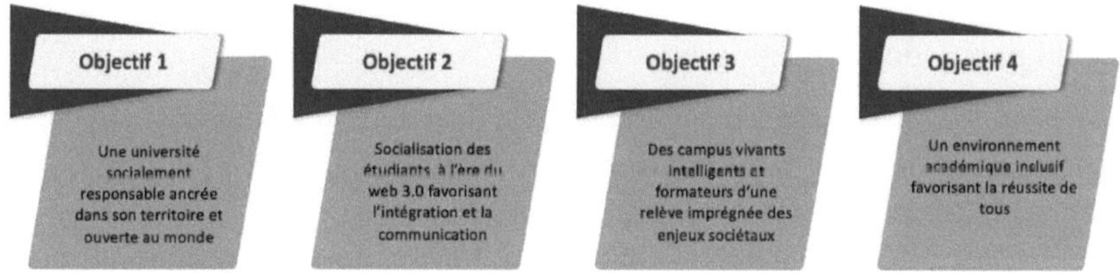

Main objective:

To create an inclusive, welcoming and dynamic university environment that promotes diversity, well-being, student engagement and successful integration into the academic and professional world.

1. Promoting Inclusion and Diversity

Inclusion and diversity are essential to enriching university life and fostering a climate of respect and collaboration.

Specific objectives :

- Increase the representation of under-represented groups in the student population.
- Promoting a culture of inclusion that respects differences.

Detailed actions:

- **Awareness campaign:** Organise awareness campaigns on cultural, religious and gender diversity, using posters, brochures and interactive events (e.g. debates, film screenings).
- **Inclusive admissions policies:** Implementing admissions policies that promote access for students from disadvantaged backgrounds, by offering bursaries and financial aid.
- **Teacher training:** Offer training for academic staff on inclusive teaching approaches and managing diverse classes.

Performance indicators :

- Rate of increase in diversity within the student population.
- Number of training sessions given to staff on inclusion.
- Feedback from students on their inclusion experience.

2. Student Involvement and Community Life

Active student involvement in community and academic life enhances the university experience.

Specific objectives :

- Create opportunities for students to get involved in enriching and meaningful activities.
- Foster a climate of camaraderie and collaboration.

Detailed actions:

- **Creation of a calendar of events:** Establish an annual calendar of cultural, social and sporting events, including open days, competitions, conferences and workshops.
- **Logistical and financial support for student associations:** Provide financial and logistical support to student associations to help them organise their activities (rooms, equipment, etc.).
- **Setting up a recognition system:** Create a system for recognising students' contributions to community activities, such as annual certificates or prizes.

Performance indicators :

- Number of events organised by students and participation rates.
- Student satisfaction rate with community activities.
- Number of student projects funded and supported.

3. Student Health and Wellbeing

Ensuring the physical and mental well-being of students is essential to their academic success.

Specific objectives :

- Provide easy access to mental and physical health services.
- Promoting a healthy, balanced lifestyle.

Detailed actions:

- **Free psychological consultations:** Establish a free psychological consultation service, with professionals trained to deal with problems such as stress, anxiety and depression.
- **Sports and leisure programmes:** Set up regular sports programmes (football, basketball, yoga, etc.) and leisure activities to encourage an active lifestyle.
- **Wellness days:** Organise days dedicated to health and wellbeing, with workshops on nutrition, stress management and physical activity sessions.

Performance indicators :

- Number of students using mental health services.
- Participation rates in sports programmes and wellness days.
- Student satisfaction rate with health and welfare services.

4. Professional Integration and Skills Development

Preparing students for working life is crucial to their future success.

Specific objectives :

•   Strengthen links with the professional sector for work placements and jobs.

•   Develop the cross-disciplinary skills needed in the job market.

Detailed actions:

•   **Compulsory work placements:** Incorporate compulsory work placement periods into curricula to provide practical experience and professional contacts.

•   **Workshops on professional skills:** Organise workshops on CV writing, interview preparation and interpersonal skills.

•   **Mentoring by professionals:** Set up a mentoring programme where professionals accompany students throughout their course, offering advice and recommendations.

Performance indicators :

•   Percentage of students who have found a work placement through ESEF.

•   Employability rate of graduates within six months of graduation.

•   Student satisfaction rate with professional development workshops.

5. Culture and Intercultural Exchange

Encouraging intercultural exchanges helps to enrich the university experience and promote mutual understanding.

Specific objectives :

- Encouraging exchanges between national and international students.
- Promoting a culture of openness and respect.

Detailed actions:

- **Exchange programmes:** Establish partnerships with universities abroad for student exchanges, enabling cultural immersion.
- **Intercultural celebrations:** Organising cultural celebrations such as food festivals, art exhibitions and language-sharing events.
- **Training student ambassadors:** Training student ambassadors to promote the internationalisation of ESEF and facilitate intercultural exchanges.

Performance indicators :

- Number of students taking part in exchange programmes.
- Participation rate in intercultural celebrations.
- Feedback from students on their intercultural experience at ESEF.

6. Communication and Information Sharing

Effective communication is essential to ensure that all students are aware of the resources and activities available.

Specific objectives :

- Improve internal communication between the administration, teachers and students.
- Facilitating access to information on services and events.

Detailed actions:

- **Centralised online platform:** Create an online platform where students can find information on available services, upcoming events and funding opportunities.
- **Regular newsletters:** Set up monthly e-mail newsletters with updates on events, wellbeing initiatives and work placement opportunities.
- **Regular meetings:** Organise regular meetings between student representatives and the administration to discuss concerns and suggestions.

Performance indicators :

- Rate of use of the online platform by students.
- Number of newsletters sent out and open rate.
- Student satisfaction rate with internal communication.

Conclusion

Strategic Area V: **University Life and Inclusion** aims to establish a culture of inclusion, well-being and commitment at ESEF Agadir. By strengthening initiatives around diversity, community involvement, student well-being, professional integration and intercultural exchanges, ESEF is positioning itself as a key player in inclusive education. This strategic focus contributes not only to students' academic success, but also to their personal and professional development, preparing them to be the future leaders of society.

Strategic Area VI :

Digitalisation

Main objective:

Taking advantage of digital tools and information technologies to improve teaching, research, administrative management and student services, while consolidating and capitalising on digital assets.

1. Improving education through digitalization

Integrating digital tools into the teaching process can make learning more interactive and accessible.

Specific objectives :

- Using digital tools to diversify teaching methods.
- Strengthen interaction between teachers and students.

Detailed actions:

- **Implementation of the flipped classroom:** Adopt flipped classroom methods where students study theoretical content online and use class time for practical activities, discussions and group work.
- **Creation of MOOCs (Massive Open Online Courses):** Developing massive open online courses on key education and training topics, accessible to a wide audience.
- **Digital resources:** Developing a rich digital library including e-books, articles, video tutorials and interactive resources.

Performance indicators :

- Percentage of teachers using digital tools in their lessons.
- Student participation rates in MOOCs and the digital library.
- Student evaluations of the effectiveness of digital teaching methods.

2. Optimisation of administrative processes

Digitising administrative processes can not only improve efficiency, but also facilitate access to services for students and staff.

Specific objectives :

- Develop centralised, digital administrative management.
- Reduce paperwork and improve application processing times.

Detailed actions:

- **Setting up an integrated information system:** Developing a centralised system for managing all administrative information (enrolments, grades, diplomas, etc.) that can be accessed by students and staff.
- **Process automation:** automate administrative procedures such as grant applications, course registrations and certificates, using online forms and digital workflows.
- **Digital customer service:** Create an online helpdesk to answer questions from students and parents, facilitating access to information.

Performance indicators :

- Satisfaction rate of users of the integrated information system.
- Average processing time for administrative requests.
- Reduction in paperwork thanks to digitisation.

3. Reinforcing Research through Digitalisation

Digitalisation can also play a key role in the development of research, by facilitating access to resources and improving collaboration.

Specific objectives :

- Improving access to research tools and resources.
- Encouraging inter-institutional collaboration.

Detailed actions:

- **Research portal:** Create a research portal to bring together all the publications, current projects and research results of teachers and students, accessible online.
- **Online databases:** Subscribe to specialist research databases to provide access to scientific journals and relevant publications.
- **Virtual seminars and conferences:** Organising virtual seminars and conferences to encourage knowledge sharing and collaboration between researchers, both locally and internationally.

Performance indicators :

- Number of publications accessible via the search portal.
- Rate of use of research databases by teachers and students.
- Number of research collaborations established thanks to virtual seminars.

4. Raising awareness and training in digital literacy

The development of a digital culture is essential to guarantee the effectiveness of digitisation initiatives.

Specific objectives :

• Promoting the importance of digital skills to the university community.

• Training staff and students in digital tools.

Detailed actions:

• **Awareness-raising workshops:** Organise regular workshops to raise awareness among the university community of the challenges of digitisation, including cybersecurity and the protection of personal data.

• **Continuing education programmes:** Set up continuing education programmes for staff and students on specific digital skills, such as data management, digital marketing and data analysis.

• **Use of collaboration tools:** Train students and staff to use digital collaboration tools (such as Google Workspace, Microsoft Teams, etc.) to facilitate teamwork.

Performance indicators :

• Participation rate in awareness-raising and training workshops.

• Feedback from participants on the usefulness of the training.

• Assessment of students' and staff's digital skills before and after training courses.

5. Capitalising on and consolidating digital assets

To ensure the sustainability of digital initiatives, it is crucial to capitalise on experience and projects already completed.

Specific objectives :

- Assess the impact of existing digital initiatives.
- Regular monitoring of digital projects.

Detailed actions:

- **Regular evaluation:** Set up an annual evaluation process for digital initiatives to analyse their impact and effectiveness, based on quantitative and qualitative indicators.
- **Building partnerships:** Working with other institutions to share best practice and resources, while participating in research projects on the digitisation of education.
- **Document successes:** Create an annual report on ESEF's digital projects, including case studies of successful initiatives, lessons learned and recommendations for the future.

Performance indicators :

- Number of assessments carried out and results obtained.
- Rate of adoption of evaluation recommendations.
- Number of partnerships established to share good practice.

6. Stakeholder commitment to digitisation

It is essential to involve all stakeholders in the digitisation process to ensure its success and adoption.

Specific objectives :

- Involve teachers, students and administrative staff in the digitisation process.
- Gather feedback to improve initiatives.

Detailed actions:

- **Creation of a digitisation committee:** Set up a committee including representatives of teachers, students and administration to oversee digital initiatives and make recommendations.
- **Surveys:** Carry out regular polls and surveys to gather user feedback on digital tools, in order to identify areas for improvement.
- **Sharing events:** Organise sharing events where teachers and students can present their positive and negative experiences of digitisation, fostering a culture of continuous improvement.

Performance indicators :

- Number of digitisation committee meetings and actions implemented.
- Response rate to polls and surveys.
- Feedback from participants on sharing events.

Conclusion

Strategic Axis VI: **Digitalisation, a lever for the development of ESEF: Capitalisation and consolidation** represents a key opportunity to transform ESEF into a modern and dynamic institution, capable of meeting the challenges of higher education in the 21st century. By integrating digital technologies into all aspects of academic and administrative life, ESEF can improve the learning experience for students, increase the efficiency of its operations, and position itself as a major player in education in North Africa and the MENA region. In doing so, ESEF will contribute to the training of competent professionals ready to meet the challenges of a constantly changing world.

This development project for the Agadir Higher School of Education and Training (ESEFA) for the period 2024-2028 is part of an ambitious and well-considered approach aimed at positioning our institution as a model of excellence in the field of education and training. In a world of rapidly changing educational challenges, we need to adapt and innovate to meet the growing needs of our society. This vision is broken down into several strategic areas, each of which plays a crucial role in our overall project.

1. Strengthening the training offer and educational innovation

We are committed to offering quality training that is adapted to the realities of the field and the demands of the market. To achieve this, we have planned :

- **Revised and modernised curricula:** By integrating cross-disciplinary skills such as critical thinking, creativity and empathy, to prepare our students to become agents of change in their future careers.
- **Active and collaborative teaching:** By promoting innovative teaching methods, such as group work, project-based learning and the use of interactive technologies. These approaches encourage the active participation of students and strengthen their commitment to the learning process.
- **Ongoing and formative assessment:** By developing assessment systems that take account not only of academic results, but also of changes in students' skills and attitudes.

2. Innovative scientific research: ESEFA's visibility and competitiveness

Research is a key driver of our development. We aim to strengthen our research capacity by :

• **Encouraging collaborative research projects:** By establishing partnerships with other academic institutions, research organisations and players in the education sector to stimulate innovation and the exchange of knowledge.

• **Supporting the publication and dissemination of results:** By offering training in scientific writing and publication in peer-reviewed journals, as well as conferences to share research results with the academic community and the general public.

• **Creating research laboratories:** By setting up structures dedicated to research, where teacher-researchers and students can collaborate on innovative projects, thereby fostering a dynamic research environment.

3. University governance: responsibility and mobilisation

Governance plays a key role in the implementation of our project. We aim to :

• **Establish participatory governance:** By involving all stakeholders in the decision-making process, including students, administrative staff and teachers, in order to strengthen transparency and accountability.

• **Develop monitoring and evaluation mechanisms:** By establishing clear performance indicators to assess the impact of our actions and adjust our strategy accordingly.

- **Promoting a culture of excellence:** By encouraging innovation and continuous improvement at all levels of the school, in order to strengthen our position as a benchmark higher education institution.

4. Strengthening cooperation, openness and partnerships

We firmly believe that cooperation is essential to enrich our educational offering. To this end, we will :

- **Establish partnerships with national and international institutions:** by promoting academic exchanges, student internships and joint research projects.
- **Working with companies and civil society organisations:** to adapt our training to the needs of the labour market and promote the employability of our graduates.
- **Organise networking events:** such as conferences, workshops and forums, to encourage the exchange of ideas and good practice between different education stakeholders.

5. University life and inclusion

University life must be inclusive and dynamic. We are committed to :

- **Promoting equal opportunities:** By putting in place access and support policies for students from disadvantaged backgrounds, and by ensuring a respectful and inclusive learning environment.
- **Developing extra-curricular activities:** By offering students opportunities to get involved in clubs, associations and community projects, thereby fostering their personal and professional development.
- **Strengthening psychological and academic support:** By providing guidance, tutoring and counselling services to help students overcome academic and personal challenges.

6. Digitalisation: a lever for development

Digitalisation is a major challenge for ESEFA. Our objective is to :

- **Integrating digital technologies into all aspects of teaching:** By developing online courses, interactive learning tools and collaborative platforms to facilitate access to information and interaction between students and teachers.

- **Optimising administrative management:** by digitising administrative processes to reduce paperwork and improve the efficiency of student services.

- **Promoting a digital culture:** By training the entire academic community in digital skills, ensuring that everyone can take advantage of the technological tools available.

In conclusion, ESEFA's development plan for the period 2024-2028 is a clear and ambitious roadmap. Each strategic axis has been carefully thought out to ensure that our institution not only responds to current challenges, but also positions itself as a leader in education and training.

We are convinced that, with the collective commitment of all stakeholders, we can realise this vision and contribute to the training of competent and innovative professionals, capable of adapting to the challenges of an ever-changing world. This project is not only an action plan for ESEFA, but also a commitment to our community, our country and future generations.

We would like to thank all those involved in the development of this project and their commitment to making ESEFA a benchmark for quality education. Together, we will build a promising future for our students and for education in Morocco.

REFERENCES

1.   Royal speeches by His Majesty King Mohammed VI

2.   National Education and Training Charter

3.   Strategic Vision 2015-2030 of the Higher Council for Education, Training and Scientific Research

4.   Law 01-00 on the organisation of Higher Education and Scientific Research

5.   The New Development Model

6.   Framework Law 51.17 on the Education, Training and Scientific Research System

7.   The 2021-2026 government programme

8.   UH2C Development Projects and Activity Reports 2002-2021

9.   Minutes of the Board of Hassan II University of Casablanca 2014-2021

10.   Reports from the High Council for Education, Training and Scientific Research

11.   National strategy for the development of scientific research up to 2025

12.   Report by the Hassan II Academy of Science and Technology: A science, technology and innovation policy to support Morocco's development

13.   Legislative and regulatory texts concerning higher education, Ministry of Higher Education, Scientific Research and Innovation, 2021

14.   Draft Finance Law 2021. Volet relatif au Ministère de l'Enseignement Supérieur de la Recherche Scientifique et de l'Innovation",

2021

15.	Regional Development Programme (PDR) for the Casablanca-Settat region

16.	National strategies for the development of the digital economy, Ministry of Industry, Trade, Investment and the Digital Economy, 08 November 2016.

17.	National Sustainable Development Strategy (NSSD) 2030, Executive Summary, October 2017

18.	Study "Profil de la croissance économique des régions", Ministère de l'Économie et des Finances, Direction des Études et des Prévisions Financières, June 2017.

Printed by Books on Demand GmbH, Norderstedt / Germany